EDGE
BOOKS™

Revised and Updated

War Planes

Night Attack Gunships
The AC-130H Spectres

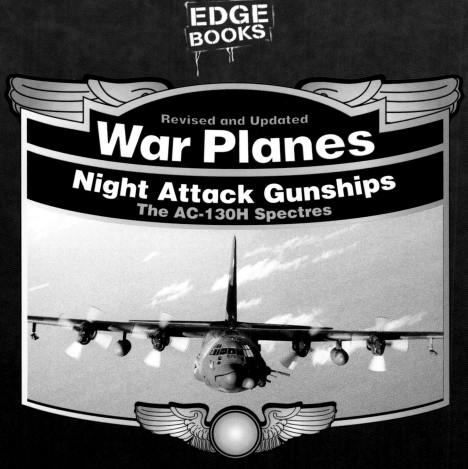

by Michael and Gladys Green

Consultant:
Raymond L. Puffer, PhD, Historian
Air Force Flight Test Center
Edwards Air Force Base, California

Capstone
press®

Mankato, Minnesota

Edge Books are published by Capstone Press,
151 Good Counsel Drive, P.O. Box 669, Mankato, Minnesota 56002.
www.capstonepress.com

Library of Congress Cataloging-in-Publication Data
Green, Michael, 1952–
    Night attack gunships : the AC-130H Spectres / by Michael and Gladys Green —
Rev. and updated.
        p. cm. — (Edge books. War planes)
        Includes bibliographical references and index.
        ISBN-13: 978-1-4296-1319-4 (hardcover)
        ISBN-10: 1-4296-1319-X (hardcover)
        1. Spectre (Gunship) — Juvenile literature. 2. Gunships (Military aircraft) — United
States — Juvenile literature. 3. Night and all-weather operations (Military aeronautics) —
United States — Juvenile literature. I. Green, Gladys, 1954– II. Title. III. Series.
UG1242.G85G74 2008
623.74'63 — dc22   2007031335

Summary: Introduces the AC-130H Gunships, their specifications, weapons, missions,
    and future in the Air Force.

Editorial Credits
Carrie A. Braulick, editor; Jo Miller, photo researcher; Katy Kudela, revised
    edition editor; Kyle Grenz, revised edition designer

Photo Credits
Aero Graphics, Inc., 25
Defense Visual Information Center (DVIC), 1, 7, 9, 10, 17, 18–19
George Hall/Corbis, 22, 26
Photo by Ted Carlson/Fotodynamics, 28
Photri-Microstock, 13, 20
U.S. Air Force photo, cover, 4

062011   006228WZVMI

Table of Contents

The AC-130H in Action

Learn about
- Need for a gunship
- AC-130 models
- AC-130 missions

A small group of U.S. soldiers is on a nighttime scouting mission in enemy territory. Enemy soldiers fire bullets at the group from many directions. The U.S. troops are trapped. They use a radio to call for help.

Soon, the enemy soldiers hear a plane flying over them. It is an AC-130H Spectre gunship. The gunship's crewmembers fire bullets in a circle around the U.S. troops.

Seconds later, the ground near the enemy soldiers explodes. Many enemy soldiers are killed or wounded and the enemy commander orders his soldiers to retreat.

A rescue helicopter picks up the U.S. soldiers. The gunship returns to a nearby air base.

Need for a Gunship

In the early 1960s, the U.S. military was fighting in the Vietnam War (1954–1975) in Southeast Asia. Thousands of trucks brought supplies to enemy soldiers. The supply trucks operated along jungle trails at night.

The U.S. Air Force needed a special type of plane called a gunship to destroy the supply trucks. The gunship had to travel long distances and stay in the air for long periods of time. It needed to fly slowly so pilots could see enemy trucks at night. The aircraft also had to carry weapons powerful enough to destroy large trucks.

AC-130H Development

The Air Force made changes to planes called the AC-47 and the AC-119 to make them more capable of defeating enemy trucks. After crews flew them successfully on missions, Air Force officials decided to change a cargo plane called the C-130 into a gunship. In early 1967, manufacturers completed the first test model of the plane. Pilots flew it on its first mission against enemy trucks in late 1967. The Air Force ordered seven final models of the gunship. These gunships were called AC-130As.

The Air Force later improved its AC-130A gunships. In 1971, the Air Force started to fly the AC-130E. This gunship had larger guns and better night-vision devices.

EDGE FACT

No other nation in the world uses gunships.

In 1967, Air Force pilots began to fly AC-130As.

In 1973, manufacturers modified the AC-130E into the AC-130H. This gunship had better communications and targeting equipment. The AC-130H also had more powerful engines than earlier gunship models.

Today, the Air Force has eight AC-130Hs in service. AC-130H crewmembers provide close air support to soldiers. They also perform missions to attack targets and to protect buildings and resources.

Inside the AC-130H

Learn about
- AC-130H features
- Locating targets
- AC-130H crew

The AC-130H is a large, sturdy aircraft. It is nearly 98 feet (30 meters) long and more than 38 feet (11 meters) tall. The distance between its wingtips is about 132 feet (40 meters). This large wingspan helps the aircraft quickly land and take off. The size of the AC-130H allows it to carry weapons and a large crew. It can weigh up to 155,000 pounds (69,750 kilograms) when fully loaded with weapons and equipment.

Protection

AC-130H pilots often fly low and slow over targets. This practice allows the crew to protect soldiers and attack targets. But flying slowly over targets is dangerous. Enemy troops can easily shoot down slow, low-flying planes. The AC-130H has strong metal plates called armor. The armor protects important parts of the plane from enemy weapons.

The AC-130H also has protection from heat-seeking enemy missiles. A heat-seeking missile has a sensor in its nose. The sensor guides the missile toward a plane's exhaust heat. The AC-130H has exhaust coverings to spread out and cool down the exhaust heat.

AC-130H crewmembers also can release hot, bright objects called flares to protect the plane from heat-seeking missiles. The missiles may follow the flares instead of the plane.

chaff — strips of metal foil dropped by an aircraft to confuse enemy radar

The AC-130H crew sometimes releases flares.

The AC-130H crew can use a radar jammer to prevent radar-guided missiles from hitting the aircraft. The jammer sends out powerful electronic signals that prevent enemy radar from working properly.

The AC-130H crew also can drop small metal strips called **chaff**. Each metal strip reflects energy to the radar station. The radar system then has difficulty locating the plane.

Engines

The AC-130H has four large turboprop engines. Each turboprop engine has a jet engine and a propeller. The jet engine turns the propeller. The turning propeller then produces **thrust**.

The engines give the AC-130H a top speed of about 300 miles (483 kilometers) per hour. The AC-130H flies slowly to perform close air support and troop protection missions.

Night-Vision Equipment

Crewmembers fly the AC-130H mainly at night. The aircraft has a Forward-Looking Infrared (FLIR) system that helps pilots see targets and surroundings. The FLIR system detects heat in objects in the air and on the ground. The location of the objects is displayed on a cockpit screen.

The AC-130H also has a radar system to help crewmembers locate targets. A second radar system detects signals from electronic sensors on the ground. These sensors can find the location of enemy soldiers and vehicles.

thrust — the force created by a jet engine

AC-130H Specifications

Function:	Close air support and troop protection
Manufacturer:	Lockheed Martin
Deployed:	1972
Length:	97 feet, 9 inches (29.8 meters)
Wingspan:	132 feet, 7 inches (40.4 meters)
Height:	38 feet, 6 inches (11.7 meters)
Weight:	155,000 pounds (69,750 kilograms)
Engine:	Four Allison turboprop engines
Speed:	300 miles (483 kilometers) per hour
Range:	1,500 miles (2,414 kilometers); unlimited with in-flight refueling
Crew:	14

The ASQ-145A Low-Level Light Television (LLLTV) system gathers light from all available sources. It can detect light that is hard for people to see. The ASQ-145A uses the light to locate objects.

AC-130H Crew

Each AC-130H has 14 crewmembers. Nine crewmembers operate sensors or are part of the weapons crew. Sensor operators use equipment to locate targets. Weapons crewmembers reload the guns and make sure they are ready to be fired.

The other five crewmembers include the pilot, copilot, navigator, fire control officer, and electronic warfare officer. The navigator helps the two pilots locate targets. The fire control officer makes sure the aircraft's weapons work properly. The electronic warfare officer protects the plane from enemy weapons.

EDGE FACT

All of the Air Force's gunships are based at Hurlburt Field in Florida.

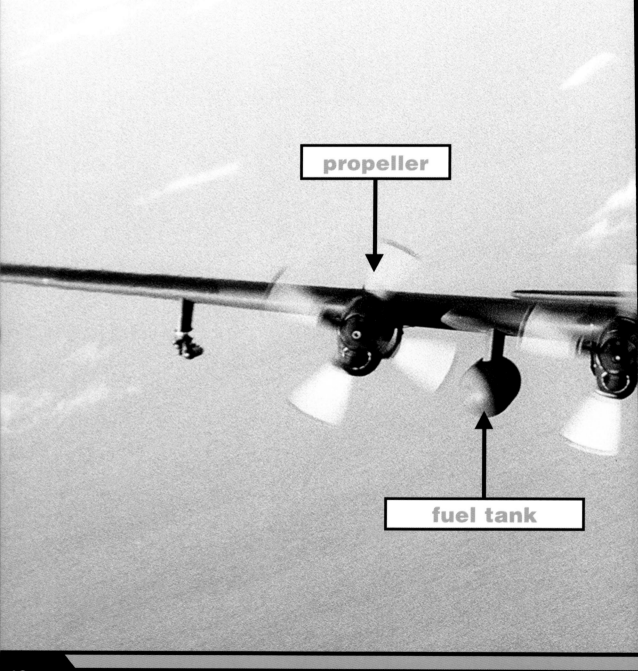

propeller

fuel tank

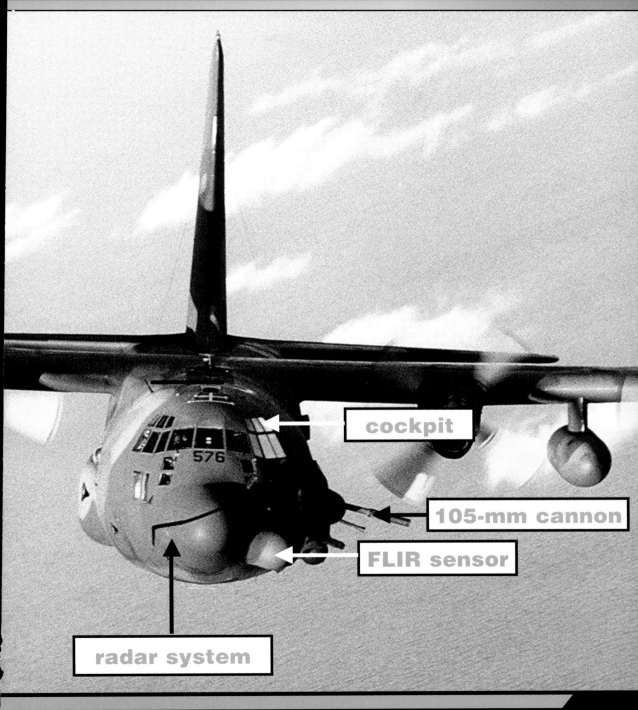

cockpit

105-mm cannon

FLIR sensor

radar system

Chapter 3

Weapons and Tactics

Learn about

- Cannons
- Fire control system
- AC-130H attack method

The first Air Force gunships had only short-range machine guns. Pilots needed to fly very low to use them. Enemy ground forces could easily shoot down the gunships.

The AC-130H has two cannons that fire large bullets called shells. The cannons are more powerful and have a longer range than machine guns.

The AC-130H's cannons are powerful.

Types of Cannons

The AC-130H carries a 40-millimeter (mm) and a 105-mm cannon. Crewmembers often use the 40-mm cannon against enemy soldiers and vehicles. They often use the 105-mm cannon against enemy tanks and **bunkers**.

The crew loads the 40-mm cannon with shells. The cannon can fire 100 shells per minute. It may fire armor-piercing shells. These shells have a pointed end made of hard steel that can punch through armor.

The AC-130H carries 100 shells for the 105-mm cannon. Crewmembers load each shell into the cannon. It can fire six to 10 shells per minute.

The AC-130H's cannons have an accurate fire control system. This system automatically aims the AC-130H's cannons. It often helps crewmembers hit targets with the first fired shell.

Tactics

Many types of aircraft can only fire weapons when they are facing targets. Forward-firing planes must turn around to make a second or third attack on a ground target. Enemy soldiers can hide or move before the next attack.

bunker — an underground shelter from bomb attacks and gunfire

The AC-130H flies in a circle to attack ground targets. Its cannons are on the left side. A circular attack pattern allows the cannons to continuously hit targets.

On protection missions, the AC-130H crew might not fire its weapons. Instead, the presence of the gunship warns enemy forces. The crew flies near the soldiers, buildings, or resources the military wants to protect. The crewmembers are ready to fire the cannons if needed.

EDGE FACT

The 105-mm cannon is the largest cannon ever fired from an airplane. The cannon's shells are about the size of an adult man's leg.

Serving the Military

Learn about
- AC-130H improvements
- The AC-130U
- Future AC-130 plans

The AC-130H has been an important part of the Air Force for more than 30 years. AC-130H crewmembers have participated in several military operations. In 1996, AC-130H crews took part in Operation Assured Response. This operation helped Americans leave Liberia. Fighting had broken out in this African country.

In 2001, AC-130H crews performed missions in Operation Enduring Freedom. This operation targeted terrorists in the country of Afghanistan.

The Air Force began to fly the AC-130U in 1994.

Improvements

The Air Force has improved the AC-130H throughout its service life. It has updated the AC-130H's FLIR, radar, and fire control systems. The cannon mounts also were redesigned to make them lighter.

In the early 1990s, the Air Force added a Global Positioning System (GPS) to the AC-130H. The GPS helps crewmembers keep track of their location.

The AC-130U

In 1994, the Air Force began to fly the AC-130U Spooky. This plane is a replacement for the AC-130A. Aircraft manufacturer Boeing built 13 AC-130Us for the Air Force.

The AC-130U has one of the most advanced aircraft weapon systems in the world. Sensors in the AC-130U's fire control system can aim at two different targets at the same time. The two targets can be up to .6 mile (1 kilometer) away from each other. No other ground attack plane in the world has this ability.

In 2001, military officials announced plans to update and possibly replace the AC-130 gunship models. The new gunship would have advanced sensors and weapons.

Both AC-130Hs and AC-130Us may be replaced in the future. Crews will continue to fly them on missions throughout the world until they become outdated.

GLOSSARY

bunker (BUHNGK-ur) — an underground shelter from bomb attacks and gunfire

chaff (CHAF) — strips of metal foil dropped by an aircraft to confuse enemy radar

exhaust (eg-ZAWST) — heated air leaving a jet engine

propeller (pruh-PEL-ur) — a set of rotating blades that provides force to move an aircraft through the air

radar (RAY-dar) — equipment that uses radio waves to locate and guide objects

sensor (SEN-sur) — an instrument that detects physical changes in the environment

shell (SHEL) — a large bullet fired from a cannon

thrust (THRUHST) — the force created by a jet engine; thrust pushes an airplane forward.

READ MORE

Doeden, Matt. *The U.S. Air Force.* The U.S. Armed Forces. Mankato, Minn.: Capstone Press, 2005.

Graham, Ian. *Warplanes.* The World's Greatest. Chicago: Raintree, 2006.

Roberts, Jeremy. *U.S. Air Force Special Operations.* U.S. Armed Forces. Minneapolis: Lerner, 2005.

INTERNET SITES

FactHound offers a safe, fun way to find Internet sites related to this book. All of the sites on FactHound have been researched by our staff.

Here's how:
1. Visit *www.facthound.com*
2. Choose your grade level.
3. Type in this book ID **142961319X** for age-appropriate sites. You may also browse subjects by clicking on letters, or by clicking on pictures and words.
4. Click on the **Fetch It** button.

FactHound will fetch the best sites for you!

INDEX